MARK HELM

One in Love and Light

Poems to Inspire Your Soul and Lift You Higher

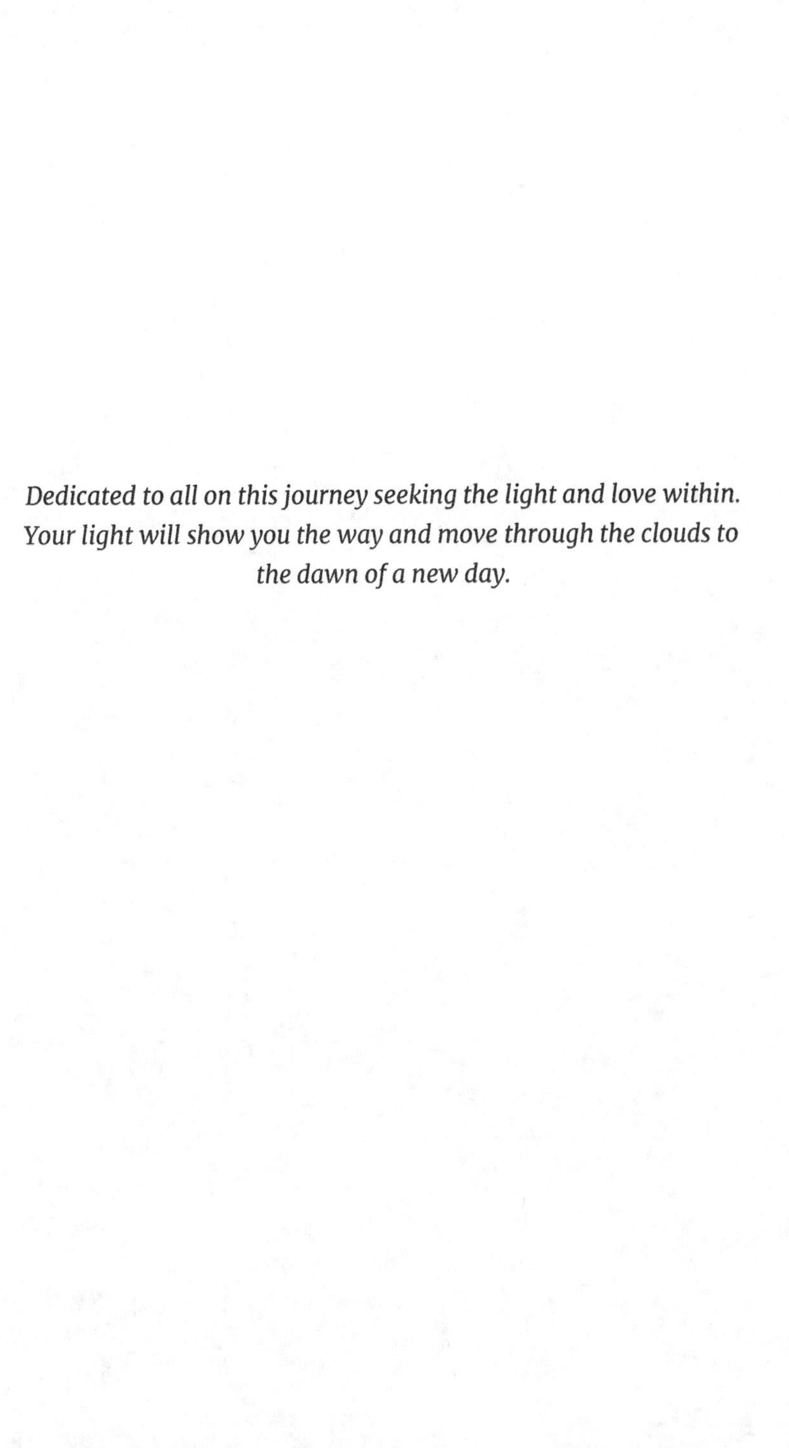

Dedicated to all on this journey seeking the light and love within. Your light will show you the way and move through the clouds to the dawn of a new day.

Every moment is made glorious by the
light of love

Rumi

Contents

Foreword

One in Love and Light are poems which speak to the love and light within you and all others for we all go as one in spirit, one with our source and creator, reminding us whatever we see before our eyes, we know eternal peace and joy are what we truly share within. As we rise each day, Love and Light will help you find your way and bring a smile to your soul for this is a choice you can behold. Remember, the light always shines beyond the clouds we travel through. We always have a choice to choose again for how we feel inside, and you my friend, will light the way for others by doing so.

Acknowledgement

To all of you who bring the light and forever shine so bright

I am one

I am one with the earth and sky
I am one with the stars on high
white puffy clouds floating which pass
and one with the beautiful blades of grass

I am one with all my sisters and brothers
with every thought we share with one another
I am one with the deep blue seas
and all therein contains you and me

I am one with as all time blends
the future, the past, the present will mend
I am one with God my creator eternal
all pain, all sorrow, all limits will end

I am one the salt of the earth
the birds that soar, the lion that roars
I am one no matter the road I travel
I am one as he holds my hand
with the tiny grains for sand

I am one with the sunlit dawn

a forest and a newborn fawn
I am one with the mighty oak
the rains which fall and the earth they soak

I am one with a drop of water in an early morning dew
a wisp of wind moving a leaf or two
a mighty volcano red hot lava
and early morning cup of java

We are one with all forms you see
in thought, in words, all is one with you and me
Love and Light are forever there too
showing the way to the truth within for me and you

Brush the clouds away

Hidden behind a wall so high
it seemed nothing ever reached the sky.
Kept inside and I could not see
what was holding the light back from me.

But he has shown
which way to go
to brush the clouds away
to a sunlit, brilliant day.

I had fears but with him near
holding my hand, always here
clouds float gently by
moving beyond, to a brilliant lit sky

Though it may seem
we are lost within the dream
that beyond the clouds lie nothing seeming
rest assured beyond lies truth, love, and all meaning

Go ahead and pass them by
one by one reaching up so high

climbing the ladder with each passing day
on our journey, as he lights our way

God is light

God is light
God is love
and you are light
and you are love
and what seems to be two
in reality is one
what fears you may have
love and light can dispel

Your brother is light
and your brother is love
for what you see is not his reality
for love and light are not separate
they hold each forevermore
they know not darkness
light shines away
so let your love forgive today

Today light shines away your darkness

Today light shines away your darkness
it spreads far beyond your sight
into everything with its might

Today light shines within you
and any sins you think you have
are vanished in an instant
and light no longer looks at them

Today light knows not fears
for when they are brought into thee
they disappear forever with its might
for such is the power and brilliance of the light

Today, for an instant
light will shine your way
and you will learn its true meaning
as it brightens up your day

And so tonight

And so tonight, with thoughts alone
I ponder, I write, within my cozy home
winds outside blow north through pines
and inside thoughts swirl, are they all mine?

A fire burns bright and embers glow on the hearth
and a mind wonders deeper for words to unearth
yes this is my time, joyful and free
a time to spin and create poems, stories, and fantasy.

And so tonight music plays softly
and fingers move swiftly
words are caught while dancing in air
in my world, there is not a care.

For its my time, and my place
a land of dreams, of timeless space
of love, and joy, rhyme and more
moving beyond the outer door.

Where they appear, I do not know
nor contemplate where they go

all I know is now there is a darkening night
and thoughts, become an awakening light.

As Day turns to misty night

As day turns to misty night
searching for peace and for the light
through it all it is your choice
to seek, to find, your own voice

By choosing the love within your heart now
and it will never fail to show you how
let your inner voice come out and show
what is deep inside your soul

Whether song, dance, or play
an artist making figures of clay
you have a part to add to the symphony
the universal song, and know, love is me

Let your voice shine so loud and clear
let it out for all to hear
be the one as only you can
let the light in you forever extend

For you have found your voice
and it was the right choice

the journey through the misty night
has once again shown your light

Awaiting the dawn of light

Early morning in Springtime rain
I wake and outside is darkness through the window pane
Shroud in a misty gray blanket covering the sky
I peer outside and watch tiny rabbits scurry by

Drops of water move down with ease
on a journey along golden green leaves
and silently in freedom fall through the air
I wonder if, they have any cares

Off in the distance a white halo glows dim
from a street lamp hidden in fog within
no sounds are made as droplets fall on the clay
and we await the dawn, of lights new day

And slowly the darkness begins to make a subtle change
black and blue then red golden light begins to appear, far across
the open range
and smiling I know with deep content inside
the light will peacefully shine away any darkness which hides

And I await the wakening dawn of light

for I know it shows the truth of our sight
and drift back off to sleep in a soft warm bed
as it all in dreams happens inside my head

Awake into the day

Awake into the day
into the glorious dawn of light
See shining in all you meet
and help make their day bright

And know that thoughts travel far
and send the light out into the world
for all will awake
from the day and thoughts you make

Smile in the joy that love will bring
that your light will heal
and the song it will sing
know in your heart each has a brand new start
for the darkness is gone
and light shows the way is won

Everything is all one

Treat everything as one
all is the same, there is nothing to blame
be kind to the smallest grain of sand
for within it we all will understand

Two plus two equals one
and within the mind we are all reborn
there are no broken pieces within
because within love they have no end

Let love light your way today
for in gratitude they show you the way

Fly away with a feather of forgiveness

Fly away with a feather of forgiveness
let go those thoughts which bring you pain
your light shines through day and night
and through the storm clouds of rain

We all go hand in hand
across this barren land
on our paths of love and light
helping each other with God's might

And know forgiveness feather is always there
to help us all in moments our soul is bare
in times we cry, in times of need
or forgiveness know it has planted a seed

Fly on through those clouds at night
whatever emotion has clouded your sight
the journey with a mighty feather
brings us peace within any change in weather

Heaven is within you now in thought not far
as we fly away through the stars

knowing earth is only a moment in time
as we move through a life of rhymes

So when times get hard and you are in pain
or anger has grabbed hold of you
reach out and touch that feather we all have
and let that thought go
and you can fly away

Know you are worthy

Focus on Now,
the past is gone
Focus on now
to show you how

Create in this moment
of time you have
create love, joy, and bliss
and on these insist

You are worthy of love
You are worthy of forgiveness
You are worthy of all goodness
Your are worthy of happiness
in each moment so you choose
to reach beyond what is seen
and see the real you

Seek not outside yourself
to feel that you are worthy
for as a son of God you already are
love and eternal light

For your are a light
your past is gone
drifting off into a sweet song
your worth is now
let it show you how

You are a shining star!

The past is gone, the morning star is shining bright
and time to move on and shine your light!
The lessons learned we are grateful for,
they showed us the way to a hidden door

We let love and laughter into our minds
and we in turn let it flow back to all to help them find
Our light shines as one further than any eye can see
Our thoughts travel to all, let that star shine back to me

I will on this day, to see my light
and I see yours shining forever in my sight
May our energy flow together as one
and on this day our light is reborn

You are a shining star!

I will be

I am not a man
and I surely can
understand I have no limits
for I am a spirit

All is given me
for in spirit
we truly have no needs
and time and space
become a place
to show his grace

I will be
what I am
and show the world
the light shines bright
rather in the day or night

I am the light, I am one

I am the light!
With no limits to see
I am the light!
Forever joy and forever free

I am courage, I am Love
I am spirit, in heaven above
I am one, in light I live
I am grateful, and freely give

I am power, I make all choices
I am within all, a chorus of angelic voices
I am in Light forever expanding
I am worthy, I am healing

I am unlimited
I am free
I am one with my God
throughout all eternity

I am one with the earth and sky
I am one with the stars on high

I am the light
forever shining so bright

No sorrow, no pain
only freedom I bring
For I am the Light
and there is no more night

The Dove of Love

Flying free up into the sky
looking at all with love from this view on high
embracing all within, knowing it is one
soaring to new heights, is the dove of love

We all fly together through any weather
for we are of the same feather
soaring ever upwards through all times
we go as one, you and I

And the Dove reaches out to help his brother fly
no matter the form, he always will try
and show the way to fly into the light
higher and higher until both are out of sight

I see Christ in you

I see Christ in you
and therefor see Christ in me
I see the Light in you
joined with the light in me

All become one
all goodness I see
held in holy love
this will I perceive

Space has no distance
time moves no more
for now has all the power
as I open its door

Innocence at last
images are past
we go together you and I
as the world, slips on by

I seek and find

I seek, I search for myself
along these many paths we go
longing for our place called home

There through the mist
through the darkness of night
Shines a beacon, a star
dawning light upon our sight

What seems without
is found within
what sight beholds
is the glory of men

But God is found
not among them
but they all have a glory
and all are called friend

All seek, and all with find
the one purpose of mind
All Love, all life

yours everlasting
beyond words, beyond sight
there will, God's will, and yours
It is the Light

Look inside

I've always thought if only they could see
what is inside, for that is the real me
Outside really matters not
What is judged should not be given thought

Look inside not through your eyes
Feel the love within shining throughout the sky
A Mighty Ray of light
showing the way through the night

And I behold the light in all
knowing inside their light is not small
and we go hand in hand through time
and love inside will always abide.

The Light shines through

Daylight breaks the dark of night
a golden ray of brilliant light
rising up, in the eastern sky
growing brighter and rising high

And what was dark
is now seen brand new
what is past
is a cleansing hue

The light shines through
and touches all
embraced by love
light answers the call

There is no I

There is no I
there is no my
there is no me
there is only we

Doubt is gone
the world is won
I am safe within
for eternity we are one

Light is here
to shine away fear
Love is all
we behold him now

The way is lit
before us now
He holds my hand
gently walking on clouds

And what seemed as two
becomes only one

I becomes we
in heavens victory

Love is always there

Love is always there.
Perhaps hidden behind what is seen
Perhaps not understood by what was spoken
To find the true meaning of it, let go of what is judged in past
Let go of any fear which may seem to be near

And feel the eternal bliss of love now in this moment
For it is true and forever is
And can be felt and shared now
Love will, show you how

All you are is all that has been
and all there will ever be
an unlimited joyful soul
which God gave meaning

The gift that I give, is one given me
for it goes into eternity
That which is perfect needs not defined
for its meaning is simple

It is, and all

We put so much meaning and effort in
defining who we are
where we are, why we are here

We seek in doing so by that which we see
To try and define me externally
But, we see amiss and inward do not seek
for to know thyself is not meek

and you need not look very far
to look within, do not hide
All you are is all that has been
and all there will ever be

an unlimited joyful soul
which God gave meaning
for you are one light above all
go now, and answer the call

Beyond the body

Beyond the body surrounded by light
Not something limited by sight
One in your energy, power, and might
Able to bring thousands of suns to shine away the night

This light is eternal and knows not of time
nor space, nor places, nor riddles and rhymes
no needs, no fears, no past to bring in
A body in light has heaven within

and know that all you brothers are one with you
sharing the one light expanding what is true
joined eternally with our father sharing
for a world which is caring

and for this moment close your eyes and feel
beyond the body and past all the stars
and all little thoughts, things you want and past mistakes
there is a much, much greater point of view

This is your light, this is the truth in you
One Light within God

eternally love so true

Know you are one

Know you are one
with God, with all
Know you are love
and always answer his call

Know you are light
Feel its power and might
Unlimited strength

Know you are peace
and feel the serenity
of your brothers hand
always within reach

Know you are always present
Feel the past and future
drift away as time lets go
and eternity is your present

Know Joy is yours
Be certain this is so
You are just to be

As two become one
in a mind so perfectly kind

We all sing in the chorus
with voice blending so perfect
harmony is heard
across the universe

Moving through the clouds

Watching the full moon rising slowly through the clouds
hidden in light, it still shines bright
as the darkness illuminates behind
and quickly climbs into the skies

As in our lives, the clouds float by
the light in behind them and rising high
and perhaps not seen for a moment
but always present
our light is always there

And seeing is one thing
but knowing is another
and feeling the light beyond our sight
will always show us love so bright

The moon reflects the light of the sun
reminding us the rays of there in darkness upon
and no matter which side of earth we are upon
light is always there for us to feel
and remember the saying

Peace be still

My Declaration of Independence

I declare I am here only to be helpful
to let my body be through spirits service
I will be joyful, happy, no matter what circumstance
I will light the way and blaze a trail through the stars
I will enter into a loving relationship with myself
and let thoughts go which are not the truth for what spirit I am

I declare true vision be my reality
Love is my guiding light
I will step outside of self-made boundaries
to join with the mind that shines so eternally bright

My past is no longer, forgiven and set free
My vision will become reality as I heal myself
I am grateful for all people, places, and things
which has brought me, to this present moment

Each person I see within the mind
is a thought of love, with no past to find
and now is all they are a present to me
and now I release and set both of us free

I am a healing thought unto the world
a minds light into all
A guide upon which light shines through
infinite, glorious, radiate, bright
For I am one, I am light!

Oh the night

In the wee hours of darkest night
my mind awakes stirred by light
and scattering thoughts become one
a time to write and be alone

The owl hoots outside the window panes
as thoughts slow from days fast lane
and oh how I love the stillness of the night
soaring words of endless delight

As a moon hides behind the clouds
winds are still and peace is found
and a world stands silently to mend
as words shape, move, and bend

Stars far off in blackened sky
remind us we are infinity, and now can fly
and touch upon that secret place
and slow down, from a worldly race

Oh the night
a time to search the soul and write

words will flow in endless delight

The Arch of Peace

Welcome my friend the the arch of peace
an arch of love forever in reach
an arch where time holds no meaning
for we understand we all are dreaming

Day in and day out our purpose become known
for what the world is, and what we have sown
for the arch is forgiveness as we make our way
to live a life in moments of joy for today

Things may happen outside and often will
but my arch is with him, and peace be still
and so dear brothers we all together stand
within an arch beyond time, holding his hand

The Dawn awakes

The dawn awakes for a day brand new
a glorious sunrise shines on the sparkling dew
Brilliant hues of light stream through the sky
Showing a new earth, and we bid darkness goodbye

And so for you, let your way be filled with light
with the sun streaming from you far beyond sight
Shining love on everything and everyone
Show that truth in you and it will be done

And as this light goes forth from you
Judge not your brother and forgive him too
For light only shines making all right
And goes on forever, one in his sight

A flash of light

I awoke one early morning
and thought of moving beyond
those many things swirling inside
and the wish for them to be gone

As I sunk deeper into the mind
letting go of past and future to not find
a flash of light appeared to me
but it was not lightening I was to see

It was a brief moment but I smiled
for I knew perhaps I went another mile
on this journey to see the light
beyond the veil were all shines so bright

and the next time I awake
I will try again to sink into this state
of letting go what seems to be
into the light of our eternity

Driving down the road of life

Driving down the road of life
down a foggy road with no end in site
On through time we travel on
with an endless riddle which game we are upon

Up ahead we see a mist
the road melts from view
Drive on through my friend they are but clouds
the roads tarry on, and will be a brighter hue

The journey goes beyond what seems like an end
and fear not my brothers for we together with love we send
beyond the clouds is our infinite circle of light
we begin to know the road travels beyond our sight

Is your light still on?

Is it still on?
Does it burn bright?
Do you see it now?
Where is your light?

Do clouds of life
seem to make it hide?
Do they pass on by
Are you looking inside?

Do you see it there?
or shining anywhere?
If you look you will find
it is there within the mind

Above the dark clouds
whispering by that shining face
The Light is always there
eternity is its place

Your Light is my light
and in him we are one

for eternity knows you now
Be still, and he will show you how

A Spark

A spark
a start
of illumination
a great ray of light
brilliant
eternal
forever growing bright

One with all
within the light
which started by sparks
soaring into the night

Each and all have this spark
find it, cherish it, be grateful
for it is the way
out of the dark

And towards that source
so long hidden
for all of time
shall be in a moment ridden

Perhaps that spark may not always show
perhaps it is covered in layers of snow
and perhaps you can see beyond your view
of a mighty spark in your brother and you

Each of us contains that thought
a spark of love eternity has brought
a spark of peace and understanding
a spark of joy and kindness

And from that spark
we join with all other lights
and cover the universe
where light has no end in sight

Tonight

Tonight in thoughts of light
A world renews beyond our sight
tonight while dreams of misty sleep
with love he eternally with us keeps

Tonight far beyond the shining stars
our light travels so very far
Tonight we join as one
and know never are we alone

Tonight love gently embraces all
for we all will answer lights call
Tonight I know the power of his might
to shine my light, so very, very bright

Trails of Light

What type of trial do you leave,
when you are flying through the sky
What love sparkles from you
and you zoom on by?

Through the Path of Love
leads each day
Those who will follow
will never loose the way

and rest assured when you lead with love
the way will always be so bright
for all will be able
to follow your light

Given a gift

You have been given a wonderful gift
you are not left in time moving adrift
Use it without guilt and build upon his plan
for showing the light beyond the man

Be glad, be joy, be one with all
Share the message of peace and love
listen to the call

Time only matters by what you learn, love, and share
otherwise, there really is not a care
He knows and guides you each step you take
Listen and remember how to create

In his love and light and laughter, I mend
this is our moment
to share the gift, which never ends

Limitations

And then God said "Let there be Light"
He did not say let there be "limits" all night
for light is not a limit in anyway, thought or form
so where did this notion of limits come from?

Know that you, yes I'm talking to you
are a being without limits too
with spirit that soars unto God
that is in fact one with him, time to all nod

All power and glory are yours
what did you do with them, did they detour?
where do you shine that given "Light"
what "limits" are you placing out of sight?

for the self is a very limiting device
a tiny thought in a land of vice
as if a little piece of space we carved and said
"this is mine, and only mine, here is me instead

and so we think we shall be
but we do not see

for eyes were made to see it not
and all they behold are tiny dots

Break free my friend from such folly
a limited space is not the right place
for the you we think is not the you he made
"Let there be light" and always it is so
There is no other place to go

Live as one Light

For the light does eternally shine
the power, and glory are yours and mine
golden, brilliant, beholden unto all
extending forever beyond a little ball

Words are but bits and pieces of it seen
for it blends all within, and time is unseen
Space no longer has any meaning
for light is here now, no need for dreaming

Live a life knowing your brother has the light
Know within him is also God's Love and might
For in truth the one all seek
is light behind a curtain do we dare peek?

Let the Light shine your past away
see that brilliant star within you today
Peace is yours, you have a choice
to let light extend beyond words voice

You have the spark to grow within
You have the Love to show

which will always extend
You know the truth

Light shines past all things

Moving beyond the clouds

Lost behind the clouds of doubt
our eyes wonder, shift, and look out
The sky seems dark, misty, gray
we journey on, day by day

But when we reach up through the sky
we will find truth when we try
and brush those clouds away in time
and see beyond for a light that shines

A brilliant light is always there
beyond those clouds, it is ours to share
Shining ever so bright, through eternity
we reach beyond and it is ours to see

And vision will change when we reach so high
clouds will be forgotten
for light streams by
and peace is found
joy abounds
all truth known
and love, always shone

Who are you?

The question posed long ago
The answer perhaps not so bold
Deep in thought, I prayed for sight
and he answered, "You are Light!"

But knowing and experiencing are 2 sides
one is a start where peace abides
by learning to let love deep inside
and let the pain no longer hide

I am by no means perfect within a man
but I try and do the best that I can
And one in him I know is true
a golden light, a brilliant hue

Who am I, the same as you
One in him, you are too
Beyond the little dust that we feel
Infinite Spirit within God I heal

For beyond what eyes can see
a brilliant light is no mystery

and Peace and Love I do find there
beyond a world with so many cares

Now I know and I understand
now I strive to be an enlightened man
for I know the journey seems long and far to reach
but with his love and mine, his will we teach

and I forgive that man who seemed little
for life is seen with such rhyme and riddles
and I forgive you as well and with gratitude say
We both are light and will within him stay

I am spirit

I am courage, I am Love
I am spirit, in heaven above

I am one, in him I live
I am humble, and freely give

I am in Light forever expanding
I am worthy, I am healing

I am power, I make all choices
I am within all, a chorus of angelic voices

Travel light

Traveling on our journey
so very far
one must travel light
to soar past the stars

We need not
take many things
for what does one need?
what should we bring?

For in what we see
in what we dream
yes we need things
but this it only seems

for we travel along
singing the same song
but someday will find
another way, for peace of mind

and the journey need not
be traveled at all

but while we go
we must have something to show

and so fellow traveler
lighten your load
let time slip away
and all the burdens of today

Let those things go
which peace brought not
and let love extend
to every thought

for you are light
eternally so bright

What is there

What is there, but brilliant light
What is one is not in sight
What takes time when none exists
What make rhymes, the poet's wit?

A journey is there, we all go on
to seek, to find and look upon
the golden light of truthfulness
the joy of, eternal bliss

What is there, is it far to reach,
or close as our very infinite mind can teach?
The question we asked
the journey undertook to unmask

What is there?

Only Love, that we share

Where is the light

Where is the light?
Is it over there?
Where can it be found?
It seems into the darkness I stare.

Where is the light?
Hidden from our sight?
A myth perhaps thought not seen
could it be nothing but a dream?

Where is the light?
Searching for so long a time
Wondering just what will I find,
when Light dawns, will I know its mine?

Where does it go?
What will it show?
How long will it last?
ah questions so many we ask

Where is your light?
It is found within

light is found in him
and it always extends
and forever love it sends

Choose this instead

Choose to marry the love within you
the good, the joy, the light inside
choose the radiance, warmth
and peace that abides

Choose to see a reflection
of the miracle with things outside
choose to forgive
and let nothing hide

Choose to make one of two
and three and four
always choose love my friend
and God will open the door

Love is already in your life
and within you
choose to realize that it is
and choose to start anew

I believe in Love

I believe in love
and for all the world to see
the depth of emotion that unites us
and keeps us with God forever to be

I believe in love
a child and the mother
a bond so strong between them
we are all one my brother

I believe in love
In God and Heaven above
through eternity it rings
of a pure snow white dove

Yes I believe in love
and I know you believe it to
For we all know peace and joy
In God, his love is you.

I just have to be me

All I am and all I am to be
is all the love that makes me
All of God is one with me
and all I have to be, is just me

Sins are gone, washed away
forgiveness dawns on a new day
guilt is past for it never lasts
and I have to be, is only me

Love is here and will light the way
now is our only time we play
and all the rest I have let it go
for Light and Love are all I need to know

Love hold nothing back

Love holds nothing seen
holds nothing back
lets go the past
lets go of things

It does keep the truth
expands to all
and hears God's call

Love gives
freely, forever
maximally
expecting nothing in return
to everyone
caring, sharing

Love is you
Love is for all
Love holds holds nothing back
and Love does not attack
for it only attracts

Love is a memory last forever

Toward the end of the long dusty trial
I can see the golden sun setting in the west
The ride has taken me all over the world
and I think I may have passed every test

And things I have had some now and then
I know at this point they don't mean a thing
because love is the only memory
which last forever, and the joy it brings

Let go in Love of the past

Let go in Love of the past
forgive and the meaning no longer lasts
like the vast ocean the sands wash away
and the light dawns upon a brand new day

Let go in Love no matter the form
it is time for the present to be reborn
and what was, is felt no longer
for love only grows stronger

The air is free, the clouds will part
and now is your time for a new start
Go in peace and move on in time
and let go now of another old rhyme

We always want more

We always want more
but do we really know what is in store?
We think that pleasures await
and the wants will open heaven's gate

Seeking and searching all the day long
and then finding perhaps something goes wrong
ah the wants of our lives the many we have had
perhaps some brought smiles and others were sad

What is one becomes two and on and on they go
it all appears to be a giant show
and we wonder when and where will I find
eternal love and our peace of mind

for that is the game
to see all wants the same
and know of the light within them all
as we bounce around a little blue ball

You are an eternal bright and shining star
and look beyond things to what you already are

Your Light is always there and so with all others
share the love we have for one another

74

Love yourself, each time you blink

As we travel through life
we find all kinds of strife
moving through time
thoughts often do not rhyme

And as I heard once from a wise sage
saying just Love and turn the page
Love no matter what you think
and love yourself each time you blink

Our world changes in all type of ways
but love holds true no matter the days
the light behind clouds may seem to hide
the seas roll in and out with changing tides

People come and go in and out of our sight
we really don't understand what is right
but remember no matter what you think
say I love myself each time you blink

And know that we all travel up the mountain
seeking the eternal joy and love's fountain

each person you meet
show kindness and love as you greet

And Love will let go of the past
and knows that it will eternally last
and Love all as one no matter what you think
and love yourself each time you blink

Reflections of Love

Children Playing
are in my memory
showing me the way
of some lost imagery

Love so strong, so complete and rare
that nothing on earth can even compare
We have all searched for that love
We have all seemed to lose our way
but search inside for true love never strays

It holds a truth we all know well
but only you, can really tell

Relationships

Dare we dream for those those that seem
what brings two together to walk through the heather
Is it magic that some suddenly appear
but then like the winds will also disappear

What will they be
Where will they go?
Questions that we all know
will begin to unfold

They start innocent and carefree
and as we know can then sail on
to places we never thought we would be

And for a time we may like where they are
or wish they were afar
for the love we share
does indeed make us care

When 2 become 1 don't we already know
that it is a race we don't have to go
for we are there already, perhaps not as we see

but one in spirit, forever to be

For any relationship be true to you
listen to your inner guide
and let your feelings not hide
open your heart
and be honest at the start

Know you are love no matter what
and one with your source
and no matter what relationships bring
they cannot make your mind change

So rather you feel up or down
or in the special place
do not blame the other
for that is the ego's race

Relationships are there to teach us
so much in time
for they can be good or not
but a lesson is surely taught
nothing can impact you if you wish
your love of God always will bring you bliss

Today I walk in Gratitude

Today I will walk in Gratitude
in all I think and do
for Love walks with me along
a path in truth where I belong

Today I think in Gratitude
of all that eyes behold
may each off its love and beauty
and judgment loosen its hold

Today I am grateful
of all that I do
For God, for me, and for all
And especially
I am grateful for you

Love comes in many forms

Remember that Love can show itself in so many forms
some may be to us clear
some may be dear
some may be in a haze
some may put in us in a daze
some may seem to be past
some may seem not to last
some we wonder why
some will make us cry

Some may seem to not involve you
always remember
Love is neither first nor last
for love is always there
no matter your past

and you are love
for eternity
and no matter what outside appears
love will embrace it all
Love is

as we answer its call

82

as we answer its call

What is love

In Heaven, love knows no boundaries and ceases to judge
On earth love can have conditions and sometimes will not budge
In Heaven, love is unconditional for one and for all
On earth, we seem to lose sight of this call

In Heaven, love is endless, joyful, and free
On earth, we at times should just let others be
In Heaven, love is peaceful, quiet, a brilliant glow
On earth love sometimes ebbs as it flows

We search our lives seeking for heavens love
Yet all the time the answer is within yet we seek without
The old saying, Know thy self is quite correct
Know that you and all others are love, and you will find rest

To forgive your brother is the reflection of heaven above
Judge them not, but love them all, and become
a Dove of Love

Your Brother

Traveling on life's lonesome highway
He reaches out a hand to hold
will you accept his gift for what it brings
or will you move beyond its ring

for he has the key
to open the door
but you must be willing
to accept him once more

If you see his gift to you
the mirror will show
that in reality
together you both go

And two have become one
and then understood clear
as being eternally joined
and heaven is here

You are Love

You are love, let it flow
across all living things
that we come to know

You are a brilliant light
which transforms any darkness,
burning eternally bright

You are joy, let it be,
for all who know you
will learn how to see

You are one
with heaven above
with all of us,
for you are love

Fall in Love with you

Fall in Love, with you.
You are the light to a shining star
The sun warming the spinning earth,
The smile to greet those near and far

You are the purpose
God shared and created you
You are the magic
You are the soul
You are the spirit

You are the love
the laughter and joy
You are the reason
for a loving season.

You are the Miracle
You are the one
You are all of heaven
in him you were born

Just for One Day

Just one day, just one moment
all the love in time and beyond
is yours and always will be
It is there waiting for you
to realize what you really are
whose heart, and soul, and being
are more brilliant than 1,000,000 stars

Love my child is never ending
Love does not hold a grievance
Love judges not your brother
and certainly not yourself
Love fills the universe
and is really all there is

God loves you and you love God
that is all that need be said
and words only reflect
the deep peace love has
in your heart it always remains

Remember my brother

who you truly are
and who goes with you on the journey
together you travel far
and love goes with you
every step of the way

Afterword

Thank you for purchasing this book and I hope some of the words and thoughts will help you on your journey. ***One in Love and Light*** was started from a series of poems I have written during some dark days of my life when my world seemingly fell apart in many ways. During a prayer to God one morning after going through these challenge and asking "Who am I?" I heard a deep voice reply "Light!".

Writing books was the last thing I thought of but I started writing each night afterward from poems, essays, and random thoughts, really whatever came to mind, I wrote about it. My book "***You are Light***" came from these writings and "***Peace Matters***" as well.

Peace, Love, and Light to you my friends,

Mark

About the Author

Mark is the father of 3 amazing children and lives near his hometown of Wylie, Texas. He loves spending time with his family and friends along with traveling, and meeting new people, and enjoys hiking outdoors and yearns to have a place near the beach. He loves to sing karaoke, with the choir, and might even put an album or two in public sometime soon.

After going through some tough years in life, a new passion emerged to share a message of living with more peace, love, and joy in your life and be aware of that light within you, and within others each day.

Love and Light to you!

You can connect with me on:
🌐 https://www.markahelm.com
f https://www.facebook.com/Livein1Light

Subscribe to my newsletter:

✉ https://markahelm.com/join-email

Also by Mark Helm

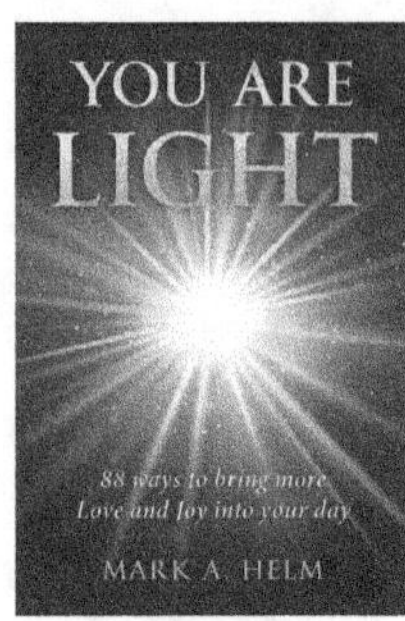

You Are Light - 88 ways to bring more Love and Joy into your day
Look at your challenges in a new light, and look at all other people in a new way since they share their light with you and you will see your light as well. Find more light each day and increase your Love and Joy step by step as we climb higher and higher and understand the truth of who we are.

YOU ARE LIGHT: 88 ways to bring more Love and Joy into your day is a guide that helps you learn how to see and feel the light from many different perspectives. Learn to uncover the darkness within by shining a little light each day to help you find your way.

Do you feel like You Are Light? Our world can show us unlimited barriers to finding the light within and we feel the darkness surround us in so many ways. We limit ourselves, we limit others, and judge all things all the time. We seek light but are not sure where to look. We look at a world of chaos and try to make sense of what is going on, what its purpose is, and what my purpose is. Where is the Light?

Peace Matters - thoughts to bring Peace within

Mark has written some ideas you can try to help you become more peaceful each day, each moment. The first step is to recognize you are not at peace which we easily do, the 2nd step is understanding you have a choice to maintain your peace or not. The power of your mind is all yours in every instance.

www.ingramcontent.com/pod-product-compliance
Lightning Source LLC
Chambersburg PA
CBHW050752160726
48004CB00002B/526